120 IDEAS FOR TINY LIVING

Acknowledgements

There are so many people who helped make this book a reality. I couldn't possibly thank everyone so here are just a few.

For Jill Valuet: Thank you for declaring years ago that neither of us could call ourselves writers if we never wrote anything. Because of you I got my act together and started put words on pages. I couldn't have done this without your friendship.

For Ryan Mitchell: I woke up on March 17, 2010 to find my story featured on The Tiny Life. If it hadn't been for you, Ryan, I would have never known that anyone cared enough to want to hear what I had to say.

For Andrew Odom: I've met a lot of people in the tiny house community but Drew has been a real inspiration and, occasionally, a partner in crime. Thanks for giving me a chance to have my voice heard quite literally.

And finally, for Matt: There aren't enough words I can say to thank you for all you have done for me. If it weren't for this crazy idea to build and live in a tiny house to begin with I could have never followed my passion to be a writer. Thank you for being my partner for all these years. There is nothing we can't do together.

120 Ideas for Tiny Living

Introduction

Whether you want to simplify your life or downsize your home there is wisdom to be found in the tiny house movement.

There is a lot to consider when deciding to make a transition to any type of alternative living situation. There are lessons to be learned from these kinds of changes that could revolutionize the way we interact with our environment and the people around us. In this book we will explore 120 ideas for tiny house living – everything from how to build it to how to decorate it. We will explore big ideas, small ideas, and everything in between.

> *"I went to the woods because I wished to live deliberately, to front only the essential facts of life, and see if I could not learn what it had to teach, and not, when I came to die, discover that I had not lived." – Henry David Thoreau*

About Life in 120 Square Feet

For all of our adult lives my partner and I felt drawn to live unconventionally. We embraced Thoreau's philosophy to "Live Deliberately." Every aspect of our lives, from sleeping, to eating, to enjoying each other's company, should be an experience. Over the course of our relationship we explored everything from traveling the country in an RV to living full time on a boat.

We looked into alternative construction like EarthShips and Cordwood Masonry. It wasn't until a friend introduced us to the Tiny House Movement and Jay Shafer's original tiny house company, Tumbleweed Tiny Houses, that a solution finally felt right. We bought land in the mountains of North Carolina and began building our tiny dream house. Working on the house took us three years as we commuted back and forth from Atlanta to Asheville. This was our adventure. We poured concrete, framed walls, built cabinets and doors. We picked out colors and storage solutions and designed specialty items to fit our needs. Every decision was deliberate. We always had to look ahead to the finished product so we understood how this puzzle would fit together. With the tiny house finished, we moved in and continued blogging about the experience.

People ask us all the time what it is like living in such a small space. Now is a good time to share some of the lessons we've learned along the way.

In this book we will explore aspects of tiny house living from the construction to exterior design to landscaping. We will check out some alternative energy systems to run a tiny house. We will look at other alternative buildings to consider. We will examine ways to organize and ways to decorate your tiny space as well as how to live there by yourself, with another person, with a family, or with your pets.

"As we live and as we are, Simplicity - with a capital 'S" - is difficult to comprehend nowadays. We are no longer truly simple. We no longer live in simple terms or places. Life is a more complex struggle now. It is now valiant to be simple: a courageous thing to even want to be simple. It is a spiritual thing to comprehend what simplicity means." – Frank Lloyd Wright

A Quick Note about Photos

All of the photos in this book, unless otherwise noted, were taken by me. I am a casual photographer (not even amateur) and I am certain the quality of the photos will reflect this. However, I decided to use my own photographs rather than hire a professional in order to maintain the authenticity of our experience. I hope you enjoy them.

1. MORNINGS IN THE TINY HOUSE

The sun rises over the mountain and I slowly wake up about 8am when the sky is already a brilliant blue. The mists that give the Smoky Mountains their name are lingering in the trees all around us. It feels like we're in a world apart from everyone else. The air is cool, no matter the time of year, and I feel a genuine sense of serenity about me.

Mornings in our tiny house are very peaceful. If you get up before the dawn you are rewarded with the most amazing sunrise through the mountains and trees; more beautiful than you could ever imagine. There are incredible shades of orange and pink without names to describe them. The chill in the air is permeable even in the heat of summer. The air is never still at these elevations.

That is how I start my day every day. Imagine being in a position to do this for yourself and your family. Imagine having a small house anywhere in the world that calls to you. What are you waiting for?

2. FRIED EGG SANDWICH

Let's start out our first Tiny House morning with a simple breakfast recipe.

Easy preparation is important for cooking in a small space with sparse resources. This fried egg sandwich couldn't be any simpler and it is so delicious.

You need:
Eggs
English muffins
Cheese (cheddar or another favorite)
Bell Peppers (I prefer green, but
you can use any color)

Toast the English muffins. We
do this using our cast iron skillet
because we do not have a
toaster. We put a little butter
on the muffins and place them
face down until they are golden brown and delicious. When they are removed we add a teeny bit of olive oil to the pan. You could add more butter if you prefer. We slice the bell peppers so they make rings about a quarter to a half an inch thick and place them in the pan until you they have a little char. Crack an egg in the middle of each ring. Cook the egg until the yolk is just the way you like it, flipping about halfway through. I like my yolks a little soft so we only cook them for a minute or two on each side. Place the cheese on the hot egg and pepper and cover the pan to allow it to melt before placing the whole thing on the English muffin. Enjoy.

3. BUILDING THE TINY HOUSE YOURSELF

With your first delicious tiny house breakfast out of the way, it is time to get down to the serious business of deciding how and where you want to build your little home.

Part and parcel of the tiny house movement is the do it yourself nature of the process. Many people choose this route because they can be in control of every aspect of their house's structure. Here are some reasons you may want to build a tiny house yourself.

- Choosing your own materials as you go.
- Being in control over the form and function.
- Designing a space that works best for you.
- Working on your own time line.
- Modifying things as you go because you figured out a better way.
- Having a sense of satisfaction that you built it with your own hands.

4. HAVING YOUR HOME PROFESSIONALLY BUILT

The second option for building a tiny house is to pay a company to build it for you. There are many tiny house builders throughout the country. More are establishing businesses every day. It is easy to find someone near enough that can consult with you and learn about your needs. Here are some reasons you may choose to have your tiny house built by a professional company.

- They are professionals. That means they have skills that homeowners don't possess and would have to learn on the fly.
- They can likely build it in a shorter time frame than if you had to learn as you go along.
- They will work with you on the design to suit your needs.
- The only anticipation you will have is waiting to move in rather than worrying about every step of the build.

5. WHEELS OR FOUNDATION

There are two choices when it comes to the foundation of your tiny house. Do you choose wheels or permanent foundation? There are pretty clear reasons why you should choose one or the other depending on your lifestyle.

Wheels offer mobility and in some cases can avoid or lessen local zoning challenges. By constructing a home on a trailer you bypass a classification as a building and become an RV or Motorhome. The structure is then licensed by the DMV or equivalent in your state rather than being subject to building

code inspections. However, other inspections might be required.

If you chose to build on a foundation, there is always a risk with this approach. Policies and elected officials can change in each municipality and so might your situation.

The other option when working with a foundation is to build a slightly larger home that is compliant with minimum size requirements within your city. This may mean you end up with a 500 square foot home rather than a 200 square foot home, but you will be able to work closely with code officials and inspectors to construct your home legally on your property. Sometimes you can build a smaller structure if there is already a habitable home on site. Creative solutions include building on family land or renting a yard.

6. Types of Tiny Houses

While the most common style of tiny house is a small, conventionally framed home on a trailer or foundation, like ours, there are other options to consider. There are countless styles one can choose for building a tiny house. I want to explore a few of them in short detail. These styles include:

- air stream
- boat
- cobb
- cordwood
- earth bag
- Earthships
- gypsy
- other mobile home
- school bus
- tree house
- underground house
- yurt

7. BOATS

Boats are probably the original and most common tiny house design. Thousands of people chose a nautical lifestyle whether it is on a sailboat or maybe a trawler docked somewhere along the coast. There are also intricate little houses built on floating foundations like the houseboat community in Sausalito California. When my aunt, who had lived on a boat for some time, saw our tiny house for the first time she felt right at home commenting that it was a lot like living on a boat. The only difference is that our boat is on a mountain.

8. COB

Another alternative building option is Cob. This is an historic building technique used in Europe over 500 years ago. It mixes natural materials from the region to create sturdy clay structures. Because cob buildings only use the clay for building they become what are essentially concrete structures or "monolithic" as some describe them. Cob is labor intensive but it is environmentally friendly and can be built to any scale. Because of the labor involved, it may work perfectly for a small structure.

9. CORDWOOD MASONRY

Cordwood Masonry is another very old building technique that has been modernized by many alternative builders in the United States.

Cordwood masonry is the method of using logs with the cut ends turned to face the exterior of the home rather than traditional, lengthwise log cabin design. The cords of wood create an extremely efficient insulation. Between the stacks of logs is a hand mixed mortar that finishes the walls. You often see individuals placing colorful glass bottles in the structure as well with this technique. The flexibility of cordwood provides infinite design possibilities. You can use it to build any size home but it would make an excellent tiny space.

10. EARTH BAG

These homes are built by filling bags with the right type of soil which are then stacked upon one another to build the wall. They are commonly used to build shelters for various humanitarian projects because they are relatively easy to construct but require quite a bit of labor. These communities will come together under a management crew and build these homes in the matter of days.

Like all of the ideas included here, these buildings can be built to any size but because of the labor involved a tiny or small house could be ideal.

11. AIRSTREAM

Jay Shafer's first tiny home was an Airstream trailer and it is a popular choice among housing rebels. However, he tells stories that no matter how much he tried to winterize, the little metal box was an uncomfortable winter retreat. Depending on where you live and what you want out of your tiny house a classic airstream can make for an amazing experience. Because of the retro vibe at its core there are so many things you can do to the interior to make it a functional and aesthetically pleasing home.

12. EARTHSHIPS

Earthships are another method of building that is intended to be self-sufficient and ecologically sustainable. They are always built with solar power and excellent water reclamation systems. The most well-known community is the Greater World Earthship Community in Taos New Mexico where there are several buildings available to rent by the night or week.

This style is built using recycled tires and rammed earth. You place the tires to create the structure and fill them with packed dirt. It is very labor intensive. The south facing part of the house is always built with large windows where you will plant an indoor garden that uses the gray water produced by the homes inhabitants. It is a truly elegant system.

13. Vardo or Gypsy Wagon

A gypsy wagon, or a vardo, is another common type of tiny house. Many people are choosing to construct updated versions of these little wagons because of their style and aesthetic. Many use bright colors and luxurious fabrics throughout. There are often intricate designs on the exterior. A vardo is usually a simple bedroom on wheels, but adding a simple bathroom and kitchen can make the structure a more functional living space.

14. RVs and Other Motor Homes

Like boats, motor homes and RVs are also popular mobile living spaces. They are often used as traveling vacation homes or by retirees who want to see the country. There is no reason why a well maintained RV can't be a permanent tiny house for an enthusiast. Because of the prevalence of RV parks throughout the country you can lead a truly nomadic lifestyle with these homes.

15. Repurposed School Bus

A more funky idea for building a small home is to convert an old school bus. Lots of individuals have done this and showcased their work on the web. A school bus is very similar to the size of an RV so by stripping the interior down to the frame it provides a blank canvas for designing something incredibly cool and to suit your own tastes.

16. TREE HOUSE

Why not live out your childhood fantasies by building your home in a tree? If you are in an area where you can take advantage of the vertical space this might be a great solution for going tiny. There are many ways to construct a tree house and many of them do not harm the tree in any way. Imagine waking up in the morning and looking out over the tree tops.

17. UNDERGROUND HOUSE

Rob Roy, leading builder of cordwood masonry homes, was also well known for underground house movement in the 60s and 70s. Building a home underground can be a great way to take advantage of the environment and potential geothermal heat. There are several ways to construct a home below the ground including burying a shipping container or doing an earth burmed home where the house is dug into a sloped area.

18. YURT

A Yurt is a Mongolian structure designed to be useful for their nomadic lifestyle. At its most basic it is a round frame covered by sturdy fabric like skins or, in modern times, canvas. Many companies are building yurts with all the conveniences of home and they can be an incredible tiny space.

In some strange way, many tiny house owners have at one time thought about living in a yurt. I wonder if this kind of nomadic dream pushes us to find ways to make this sort of lifestyle really work in our lives.

19. THE MODERN TINY HOUSE

Now that you know what you want to build, how do you want to build it? There are countless options when it comes to the overall look of the house and some of the styles will inform the overall design. Many of the designs I gravitate toward tend to be either modern or rustic and sometimes a strange combination of both.

Typically, modern is demonstrated with clean lines, white accents, and glass or metal trimmings. Use metal as the uprights for your ladder. Install metal or glass shelving. Use white on your walls but add a pop of red on the sofa or bed. The Swedish furniture giant Ikea can help you design a great modern place with simplicity and keep it very user friendly.

20. THE RUSTIC TINY HOUSE

A second common house style is rustic. This is like the quintessential log cabin with lots of wood and natural elements. Usually it had warm colors such as browns and oranges. Sometimes it may also incorporate frontier or Southwestern motifs.

You may consider building a porch railing using branches for the balusters. You may incorporate natural motifs with stencils. Use bare wood and warm fabrics throughout.

For a tiny house design it may be fun to play with a combination of these two styles and design a modern rustic house.

21. WHERE TO PARK OR BUILD

Where to build or park your tiny house is a key question for any small building project. It is not one that is easily answered. You need to answer three simple questions to determine what is right for you.

- Do you want to be mobile?
- Do you want to be in a city?
- Do you want to be in the country?

Depending on the lifestyle you want and the reason you're building a tiny house in the first place your answer will vary.

Many people will build their home in the back yard of a family member or in their own back yard if they already have a home. Or if you choose to build on a foundation, like we did, you will want to have your land already, of course.

A tiny house on wheels allows for many parking options. You can rent backyard space which you may be able to find on Tiny House Listings. Or you can find a spot in a remote area and live there. There is some debate in the community about RV parks. Some are allowing tiny houses and others are still considering the issue.

Check your local building codes and RV Parking requirements before you set up shop anywhere.

22. TINY HOUSE IN THE CITY

There are many places you can park your tiny house and many people build with the intention of living in the city. The city presents its own challenges with the building codes. I interviewed Macy Miller of Mini Motives for the Tiny House Listings website and she gave some pretty good advice about dealing with codes. You should be able to approach the city government to talk about what you can do. Ultimately, once the house it built it will need to be registered with the DMV or equivalent in your state as an RV or Motorhome. This will change the legal status of the house and you will find some places you can park it. There are many ways to have a tiny house in the city, sometimes you just need to be creative about it.

Photo by Marie Mosley.

23. TINY HOUSE IN THE COUNTRY

Having a tiny house out in the country is a different concept altogether. Often, rural areas will have a much more relaxed attitude. There are areas of the country where you might not be so far out of town that it isn't worth it.

We made the choice to build our home in the mountains. We made friends with our neighbors, which was easy to do since they are all so wonderful, and let them know exactly what we were doing and how we were doing it. We even shared our systems with them so they could see how the gray water and composting worked.

"Have nothing in your houses that you do not know to be useful or believe to be beautiful." - William Morris

---

24. Types of Windows

Here is a funny story. Years ago, when we bought our plans from the Tumbleweed Tiny House Company we were told that the windows recommended were standard sizes. So we framed the house according to plan before purchasing the windows themselves. When we got to the point where we were ready to buy the windows we discovered that standard sizes differed throughout the country. We considered our options and decided to invest in custom windows.

We chose double hung windows for our home. We wanted to be able to open and close the windows in a manner that was safe for our cat so she wouldn't push out the screen and escape. We thought we might open them from the top which we actually don't do but it is nice to have the option.

We chose a hand cranked awning style for the lofts.

What are some other window styles you could choose?

- Casement Windows
- Awning windows
- Double hung
- Picture window
- Gliding window
- Skylight
- Bay window

Many tiny house builders also choose to repurpose old windows they find at antique shops, thrift stores, or reclamation stores.

25. BUILDING YOUR TINY ROOF

How to construct your roof is as big a decision as how to frame the walls of the house or whether or not to build on a foundation.

Your roof can be a simple A Frame roof, be peaked with gables, or be a sloped shed style roof. There are pros and cons to any choice. Let's look at the options.

- The easiest is the simple A Frame. A builder will explain the proper formula for you to use to have the correct angles. It is straightforward to frame and sheath because it is two straight lines.
- Additionally you can add gables and dormers to your roof.
- A shed style roof would have been our second choice. Because of the style house we built with the loft it was not practical for us, but a simple one plane roof that slopes would be great for collecting rain water. You could also put a beautiful bank of windows just under the eaves for a great view from the loft.

26. A TINY PORCH

We built our tiny house porch as a separate stand-alone deck in front of the house. It is connected to the house by the porch roof overhang. We used deck block to level the tiny deck and it took just a couple of hours to construct the whole thing. The overhang was attached to the house using a beam and bird's mouth cuts on 2X4s. This was covered in the same roofing material as the rest of our roof. We used beautiful cedar 4X4 posts to create a lintel and posts to connect it to the porch proper. We added two small stools made out of reclaimed barn wood. A red and blue garden gnome stands guard at the door. You will meet him later in this book.

27. YOUR EXTERIOR SIDING

How you want the exterior of your tiny house to look is purely a question of aesthetics. Do you want something more modern, more traditional, or more rustic? There are many possible options to consider.

- **Cedar shingles.** This classic material will give your house an adorable cottage look. Naturally resistant to rot and insect damage, cedar is a hardy material that stands the test of time.

- **Metal.** A more industrial feel can be achieved with corrugated metal. Done properly this can be maintenance free as long as you like the look of weathered metal.
- **Clapboard.** This style is an iconic look for many tiny homes. It is a good balance between labor and cost.
- **Board and batten.** This traditional country style is made using vertical boards where the joints are covered by smaller battens. Some builders replicate this technique by siding the home with stained plywood and covering the seams with 1x2s.
- **Reclaimed materials.** Another option is to look at reclaimed wood or other materials to side your house. Barn wood is a common option. Also, imagine a tiny house covered in old license plates!

28. YOUR INTERIOR WALL COVERING

Finishing the interior of the house is as important as deciding how to finish the exterior. Here are some ideas for interior finish.

- Bead board
- Pine or cedar siding
- Drywall

You may also choose a combination of these with a chair rail and drywall. Depending on how you choose to finish your house you can decide on colors and other decorative touches. Many traditional tiny houses use tongue and groove boards for the interior walls.

"Too many people spend money they haven't earned, to buy things they don't want, to impress people they don't like." – Will Rogers

---

29. Tiny House Furniture

When furnishing your tiny home you need to make sure that all the pieces are not only comfortable but small and functional. You aren't likely to be able to fit a Lazyboy recliner in the space so think carefully about how you want to plan the placement of your furniture in your tiny house. I believe that a small space only needs a few select pieces of furniture to make it complete. Regardless of what you choose for your home it needs to speak to you and make your space a comfortable, everyday retreat.

Many tiny house builders get not only their inspiration but also their furniture from Ikea. Simply walking around their showroom and looking at the ways they can fit pieces into their small space exhibits is enough to get the tiny house dreamer's creative juices flowing.

30. Sofa in the Tiny House

Seating in the tiny house can be difficult. We went through several ideas before settling on our solution. Many people build their own sofa into the design of the tiny house. We did a hybrid approach. We found a tiny dorm style futon with a frame that didn't work for us. We built a frame out of 2x4s and re-bolted the seat on top. This also allowed us to have storage underneath. This sofa is comfortable and works great in the space.

You can be as creative as the space allows for your tiny house seating. Other options include:

- Small sectional sofa
- Built in seating within a bay window area
- Futon
- Pillows and cushions on the floor

31. DIRECTOR'S CHAIRS AS STOOLS

Before moving into the tiny house we owned a set of directors' chairs. It struck us that we could remove the arms and use them as stools, which made us feel rather smart. They are very comfortable and I spend much of the day there typing since I work from home. Directors' chairs are small and take up very little space plus they can be easily folded and stored if necessary. What are some other dining chair options for tiny houses?

- Stackable chairs
- Desk chairs on wheels
- Folding butterfly chairs
- Bar stools

32. DINING TABLE

Our dining table is one of our favorite things in our tiny house. It was one of the first accessories we bought. Several other tiny house builders also use the same table. This wall mounted folding table, called a Norbo, is available at Ikea. It is exactly the right size to fit between the two windows.

There are a lot of potential options for tiny house tables. You can buy one commercially or you can make one yourself. Here are some other options tiny house builders have chosen.

- You could mount half of a salvaged or repurposed table to the wall to create an interesting look.
- Build a bar/desk/table into the wall just as you would a counter top. This would provide multiple uses.
- A table that folds up into the wall vs. down like ours.
- A very small stand-alone table.
- A table with removable legs that can be stored away.

33. YOUR CHOICE OF BED

Your bed is going to be one of the most important decisions you make in a tiny house. When we began building our Tarleton the suggestion made by the Tumbleweed Tiny House Company was to build a bed out of foam. We decided we wanted something different. Our original plan was to use an air mattress but decided against it. In fact, we spent two months sleeping on a double high air mattress while visiting family for the holidays and were very glad we didn't use one in the tiny house. Instead, we invested in a futon mattress. We placed it up in the sleeping loft and it is a perfect fit and very comfortable.

Other ideas for tiny house beds include:

- Murphy bed
- Slide Away Bed or trundle
- Futon (mattress or full pull out couch style frame)
- Tatami Mat
- Conventional Mattress
- Air Mattress
- Foam Mattress of your own design

"The minute you choose to do what you really want to do, it's a different kind of life!" - R. Buckminster Fuller

---

34. IMAGINE SPRING AT THE TINY HOUSE

Spring on our mountain is inspiring. The bright green leaves begin to sprout on the tree branches and the animals emerge from winter in the Smokies. Spring is the time for projects on the land for us. Time to plant a garden. Time to work with the spring water to make sure it is optimal. Time to clean up after any winter storms.

A couple of years ago I planted daffodils near a garden statue. When they push their new green leaves from the ground and slowly open their yellow petals to face the sun, I know that winter is nearly over. Plant your favorite bulbs near your tiny house to give yourself the same sense of renewal each year.

35. MID-DAY AT THE TINY HOUSE

It is time to take a break. Put aside your work and your chores and spend some time relaxing. Fix yourself some lunch and think about how the rest of your day will look.

When I am working from my tiny house I'm usually done with my writing by about midday. I often take short breaks to tackle some of my chores such as emptying the gray water or filling our water filter. These things help me stay connected to our tiny life.

How would you spend your days if you lived and worked from your tiny home? What are the things you've always wanted to do? Will you be on or off the grid? Will you be living with someone else or by yourself? All of these are things to consider when deciding to go tiny. Now is the perfect time to consider these questions and more.

36. PLOUGHMAN'S LUNCH

I've never been a fan of sandwiches. I don't mind a nice Panini now and again and occasionally I will occasionally eat a sub but I don't *prefer* a sandwich. Lunches were always complicated for me when I was working – I hated every option I could think of. It was really a shame that I didn't think of this idea while I had a full time job.

What I do love are antipasto or charcuterie or cheese plates. Or, as a friend called them, ploughman's lunches. Rural workers would take cured meat, a chunk of cheese, and hearty bread in the fields with them when they worked. The options are endless. Here is a typical lunch for me.

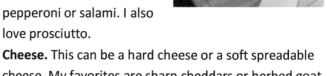

- **Cured meat.** We pick out different dried sausages each trip to the store but typically it will be a pepperoni or salami. I also love prosciutto.
- **Cheese.** This can be a hard cheese or a soft spreadable cheese. My favorites are sharp cheddars or herbed goat cheeses.
- **Crackers or bread.** I prefer the crunch of crackers so I won't typically get just a loaf of French bread but that is an option. I like bagel chips or any type of organic cracker.

37. THE HOME OFFICE

Lots of people ask us about working in the tiny house. One blog reader wanted to know how I had space for a home office to include printers, books, paperwork, etc. For us, working in the tiny house was all about changing our entire concept of "working." I am a freelance writer. Most of my work is done on a computer and submitted through the internet. I do all of my research on line as well. Therefore, the only tools that are essential for working are my laptop and an internet connection. My home office is housed in my laptop case where I store my computer and all the associated cables and other random chargers and items. I do, of course, have a pen and one small notebook to write down things the old fashioned way.

38. INTERNET IN OUR OFF THE GRID HOUSE

In conjunction to working in the tiny house people also wonder how we have an internet connection. Of course, if you have a tiny house on the grid this is not an issue and you can get any sort of service. People sometimes think that since we live off the grid and up on a mountain that we can't have internet. We actually use a wireless internet hotspot available through my cell phone provider. All of the major carriers offer these services and they are affordable. We ran a wire through the wall and it connects the wireless hotspot to a magnetic antenna that sits on our metal roof thus creating a giant antenna. We have 4G signal on our mountain.

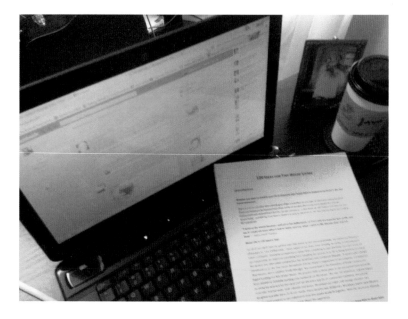

39. Social Media for the Tiny House

This seems like a strange topic, but I have put a lot of thought into the best way to handle social media from the tiny house. I realize that I am not a pioneer roughing it along the Oregon Trail, rather someone who wants to live a simple life combined with technology where it fits. I love the fact that we are off the grid but I couldn't stand to live without my internet connection.

Lots of tiny house owner's blog and promote their own story on the internet. LinkedIn is an essential network for building my business. Facebook is great for keeping up with friends, family and other like-minded individuals. We are far flung but because of the internet I know tiny housers from California, Idaho, Georgia, Florida, Oregon, Michigan, and dozens of other places. We stay connected on the internet because we can. We keep in touch because we all care about transforming our lives through simple living. All of us have very different reasons for wanting to do what we do, but we are able to come together to share ideas and our stories with one other. It reinforces our community. No one is truly alone with social media to bring us together.

As you simplify your life, the laws of the universe will be simpler; solitude will not be solitude, poverty will not be poverty, nor weakness weakness. -Henry David Thoreau

---

40. SOLAR POWER SYSTEM

When we started our tiny house build we had a small solar panel set up with small portable batteries. While this worked fine on a temporary basis but to live in our tiny space full time we needed to amp it up, no pun intended. We replaced our temporary 60 watt solar panel system with a new Kyocera 490 watt system. This consists of two 245 watt panels that connect to 45 amp Tristar MPPT charge controller made by Morning Star. These feed into three 110 amp hour AGM batteries. We used the same trusty 1800 watt inverter from our original system to convert all the power to AC inside the house. There are separate breakers throughout the system so they can be safely isolated and serviced at any time.

All of the wiring runs underground in rigid conduit.

We had bought a traditional pole and top of pole mount for the panels but we wanted more flexibility to move them since the sun varies in position in our clearing throughout the year. Matt custom designed a mount that allow us to do this as necessary.

We bought everything at the AltE Store online and they were quite helpful throughout the process.

41. ARTIFICIAL WETLAND

Years ago, when we first decided that we wanted to build something sustainable in the mountains of Western North Carolina, we found a book called *Healing Appalachia*. In it were tons of great ideas for environmentally friendly systems that you could use to improve your own patch of the Appalachian Mountains. I hope that wherever you are in the country that you might be able to find similar local resources.

One idea stuck with us: building an artificial wetland. This system is intended recycle any gray water you generate from your off the grid home. We have a 5 gallon bucket that hangs beneath our shower drain and all water that is used for cleaning ourselves or dishes is collected there. We use biodegradable shampoos and soaps to keep as many chemicals as possible out of the watershed. Each day we remove the bucket and pour it into our artificial wetland. It cycles through the series of rocks and empties out at the edge of the woods.

Our design is modified to fit our space and our aesthetics. The idea is still the same – water goes through layers of pumice, river rock and pea gravel which helps filter it before it goes into the ecosystem. We chose to us a series of pots in descending size connected by rigid pipe. This is not only a functional system but an attractive one as well. Depending on your situation you may be able to connect a hose directly to your system.

42. HYDRO POWER SOLUTIONS

We have often thought of ways we might be able to make use of the spring on our land besides just using the water. Even with our limited water flow power can be generated by installing a micro-hydro power system. If you build or park your home on land with a river or stream you may be able to generate a substantial amount of power.

There are several ideas for constructing homemade hydro power solutions available on the internet.

43. Rain water catchment

If you don't have or want to use spring or well water for your off the grid tiny house, another popular option is rain catchment. This is something we plan to do on our own tiny house but because we have access to spring water we haven't rushed to build it.

The roofing material that we purchased is coated with a food grade finish which will allow us to collect water that is ultimately potable. We will install gutters on either side of the house that will lead into a rain catchment barrel. In colder climates you may need to bury the barrel below the frost line to prevent the water from freezing.

44. Wind Power

I never thought of wind power as a reliable source of energy for a tiny house. It seemed as though the cost of the equipment to produce it would be entirely unreasonable for someone choosing to live a more simple life. That was until I learned about portable wind turbine technology. There are several models designed for and marketed to the RV communities. Some even have telescoping mounts which make set up and take down extremely easy.

Smaller wind turbines have become increasingly more affordable over the last few years. It might be worth looking into if you are in an area where you can make great use of the wind's power.

"The true way to live is to enjoy every moment as it passes, and surely it is in the everyday things around us that the beauty of life lies." – Laura Ingalls Wilder

45. YOUR TINY BATHROOM.

A bathroom is often taken for granted in a traditional house but there are some additional considerations when constructing one in a tiny home. Some of these can feel like insurmountable obstacles in a small space. Here are some of the things to take into consideration for your tiny bathroom.

- Bathroom Doors
- Shower
- Toilet
- Storage

46. YOUR TINY BATHROOM DOORS

If you have enough space in your home you may want to install a sliding door.

We decided to make two small doors that close together in the middle. This solves a couple of problems. A full size door would bang into the cabinets when it is open. With two doors it is easy to access the bathroom even if someone else is in the kitchen.

At one time we thought about curtains for the bathroom door but decided it would not provide enough privacy or enclosure for the space. I had also really wanted to do swinging western saloon doors, but the design just wasn't right. Bifold closet doors might have worked as well.

Consider how your bathroom is situated in your house. What makes sense for the space? Is it better for the door to swing in or out? Can you use a traditional door, a pocket door, or a folding door?

47. Showering in the Tiny House

Since we made the decision to leave out plumbing (for now) we needed have a solution for how to take a shower inside. In the time we spent building and camping near our tiny house we tried every kind of outdoor shower you can imagine. We used a submersible pump. We used a copper coil water heater. We used gravity fed bags. We used a Coleman hot water on demand system. All of them were good, but none were perfect.

Then Matt met a man who lived on a boat and used a simple garden sprayer for his shower. We thought this was a great idea, but there might be a way to improve it.

We found ourselves searching the local home improvement stores to buy a garden sprayer, a shower nozzle attachment and some plumbing parts to fit them all together. The sprayer we found has an on/off switch so we can take an old fashioned boat shower – turn on the water, get wet, turn off the water, soap up, turn on the water, rinse, repeat. It is amazing how much water is wasted in a traditional shower configuration. Our daily water use is pretty minimal.

Since we don't have a hot water tap we use a slightly more old fashioned method for heating our water. We fill the 2 gallon sprayer with about a gallon of air temperature water. Then we fill our kettle with about a half-gallon and heat it on our stove. Once it boils we add it to the water already in the sprayer, screw on the top, shake and pump. The final outcome is a delightfully air pressurized and hot shower. A gallon and a half is enough to get everything quite clean and I usually get a few relaxing moments to luxuriate in the hot water.

Showering is no longer just a shower, it is an experience.

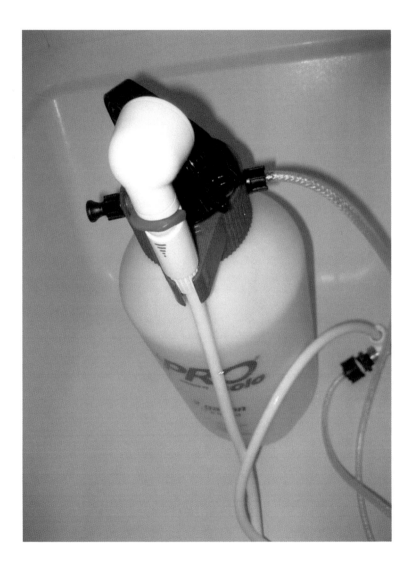

48. THE TINY HOUSE TOILET

No one wants to talk about it, but the subject is important: toilets in the tiny house. Many tiny house builders go with a dry composting system as described by Joseph Jenkins in *The Humanure Handbook*. There are also commercially available composting toilets that you can install which do the same thing but in a more technologically advanced way. I have also seen other bloggers mention an incinerating toilet which I find most fascinating.

The best part about building a composting toilet is being able to create one that fits your space. You can include a toilet paper holder and a storage bin for the cover material.

I am not an expert on humanure. If you're interested in learning more about how it works and why it is perfectly safe, I highly recommend checking out the book by Joseph Jenkins.

Other options for tiny house bathrooms include commercial composting systems, incinerating toilets, and traditional plumbing. All will require specialized systems to install and work properly.

Simplicity is an acquired taste. Mankind, left free, instinctively complicates life. - Katharine Fullerton Gerould

---

49. A TINY KITCHEN

Designing your tiny house kitchen involves the art of spatial relations. With such a small prep area you need to make every space count and be as efficient as possible.

We chose to make standard counters with cabinets beneath and used open shelves for storage above the counters. Everything in the kitchen is functional. There are four drawers beneath the two smallest counters and three shelves in the largest cabinet. The final cabinet is for refrigeration where we use a small cooler. In order to keep the space open, we chose not to build upper cabinets

Everything on the counter should be decorative as well as useful. With two people in the kitchen it may seem cramped at times, but you can expand some of the food preparation to the table.

50. Tiny Utensils and Other Easy to Use Kitchen Gadgets

Utensils are necessary but they often take up a lot of space. Use collapsible items as much as you can – they are becoming quite popular. We have collapsible set of measuring cups which stores flat as well as a collapsible calendar for draining pasta and washing vegetables. An immersion blender can be a valuable space saving tool. We also like pots and pans that nest. They are made for camping but work very well for tiny houses. Make sure everything in the tiny house has a place where it belongs or else the clutter will start to get out of hand.

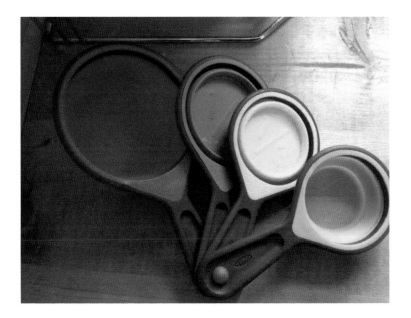

51. HOW TO USE REFRIGERATION

There is a movement outside of the tiny house community to reduce our dependence on refrigeration. Even families living in suburban homes are trying to live without using their refrigerator to store foods.

When we had a refrigerator we found that it was typically filled with half used condiments and not much else. We would often bring left overs home with us and not eat them. By choosing not

to have a conventional refrigerator in the tiny house we have become more conscious about the amount of food we cook or that we order in a restaurant. If you eat food within a few days of purchasing it many things such as fruits or vegetables can go without refrigeration. Even butter and eggs don't need to be kept too cold. Make sure you have a cool, dry place in your home. For  us, our cabinets never get very hot even on the warmest days. We also have a cooler inside the house which we can add ice to as necessary. The truth is, we rarely use it.

52. STIRLING ENGINE COOLER

The one piece of refrigeration technology that we do have is a Stirling Engine Cooler. This cooler was manufactured by Coleman, the camping equipment company, primarily for use by long haul truckers and fishermen. It is the size of a traditional cooler and has an engine called a Stirling Engine. It is a very efficient engine that cools anything stored inside. We kept the cooler under the house and power it through our battery system directly. We only turn it on when necessary. We primarily used it to cool our craft beer. While the cooler is no longer made by Coleman, there are other similar units that are still used on boats which might be a good fit for tiny spaces.

53. Cooking in the Tiny House

Cooking in the tiny house presents its own set of challenges. Many people dream of the large kitchen with the top of the line appliances. While many tiny house builders will install small versions of regular kitchen appliances such as a refrigerator or a stove, we chose to go a different route. Since our home is completely off the grid we decided to use butane burners for our general cooking and it works out very well for us.

To make the best use of space, we also built an outdoor prep area. This gives us an opportunity to spread out a bit.

54. TINY SPICES

Even an amateur cook needs access to herbs and spices. One option is to grow an herb garden to have fresh flavors, but sometimes jars of spice will do the job. Consider all the decorative ways you can display your spices.

- Fasten small mason jars or baby food jars under your cabinets of shelves. Then you can simply unscrew the jar to use the contents and put it back when you're done.
- Create a small niche in your interior wall between the studs to stack your spices.
- Put your spices in small metal containers and use a magnetic strip on a vertical surface.

55. USING CAST IRON COOKWARE

The single best weapon you can have in your tiny house kitchen arsenal is cast iron. In fact, I would recommend cast iron to anyone who wants to live, cook, and eat simply. Cast iron is extremely user friendly and perfect for a home where you are very careful about your water usage like ours. Properly seasoned cast iron cookware requires very little cleaning. Once you have finished cooking in it, clean out any obvious food particles and then rub it with a little oil and it is ready to go for the next time. I recently read an online tip that suggested using coarse salt to clean it rather than soap.

We have three essential pieces of cast iron: a wok, a skillet and a Dutch oven. We chose a skillet and Dutch oven set where the skillet can double as a lid for the Dutch oven as necessary.

56. THE CAST IRON WOK

We invested in a nice cast iron wok. As I mentioned in the last idea, cast iron is great because it is easy to clean and the food cooked on it tastes amazing.

Stir-frys are easy because there really aren't any rules. Use whatever you have. What kind of vegetables did you get from the farmers market this week? They can be stir fried. If you have left over rice and an extra farm fresh egg you can make fried rice the next day. The fresh meats and vegetables from the local farmer's market are great for this style of cooking. You can cook in your wok every day and make a completely different meal each time.

57. Easy Stir Fry Recipe

Ingredients:
Small strips or cubes of chicken or beef.
Vegetable oil
Chili Oil
Corn Starch
Honey
Ginger
Soy Sauce
Broccoli (or any vegetable you prefer. I like broccoli because it holds the sauce and is very flavorful)
Brown rice

In a separate pot, start your rice according to package directions. Bring it to a boil and then turn it down to simmer for about 40 minutes or until tender. Wait the full 40 minutes, though, because you don't want to lift the lid of the pot very often.

In a small bowl combine soy sauce and water for the base of the sauce. We do this without measuring specifically, but typically it is a half a cup of each. Add ginger and honey to taste. Stir. Add a *very* small amount of chili oil. It goes a long way and can easily ruin the sauce if too much is used. You can always add a drop or two more as you go. Then whisk in cornstarch until the sauce is thickened slightly. Again, you do this by sight.

Go ahead and chop your broccoli.

When the rice is almost done, or done and kept warm, fire up your wok. Once it is heated, drizzle with a little vegetable oil to coat the cast iron. Throw in your chicken first – this will take the longest to cook and needs to be cooked until it is no longer pink inside before you add the broccoli. Beef will take less time and you can cook it to the temperature you prefer. Once the meat is done, throw in the broccoli and the sauce. Stir it up and place the lid on the wok. Give this just a couple minutes to steam and your sir fry will be done. Serve over rice.

58. No Unitaskers in the Tiny House

I am a big fan of Alton Brown and his Food Network cooking show Good Eats. On the show he preaches that no tool in the kitchen should be a single task item. Nothing should have only one job. This is essential advice for the tiny house. There is no point to having 16 items that do one task each when you can replace it with one item that does 16 tasks. Consider your kitchen needs before stocking it. What kinds of things do you cook? What you enjoy doing in your kitchen? What kinds of food requirements do you and your family need? For example, we owned a garlic press but realized we could easily chop garlic using the same cutting board and knife we use to chop vegetables. Simplicity is key when it comes to tools in your tiny kitchen.

59. BUTANE BURNERS

Many people will build their tiny house with a small kitchen range like those used in RVs. Since this was our first time building anything we decided that we didn't want to install any appliances. We chose to build straight forward cabinets and counters and use stand-alone items for our cooking. We have a camp oven, which can only be used outside, but for regular stovetop cooking we use butane burners. Butane is efficient and the little burners work quite well. We use them for everything from heating showers to cooking dinner. The best part about the butane burners is that they are portable

Other options for indoor cooking include

- Stoves designed for RVs or Boats
- Alcohol burning stoves
- Electric hot plates
- Induction burners

60. Tiny Dishes for a Tiny House

Determining how to store your dishes may be an interesting challenge. We opted to create open shelving using shelf brackets with a modern industrial design. Our dishes came from Ikea and because of their oval shape they are able to fit on skinnier shelves. We chose white so they would match any décor.

What other options exist for dishes in the tiny house?

- Vintage China
- Mismatched plates from thrift stores for a shabby chic look
- Match the dishes to your color scheme
- Camping dishes for a rustic look
- Earthenware produced by a local artist

61. STAYING CAFFEINATED IN THE TINY HOUSE

Before moving into our tiny house we used a Keurig coffee maker for all of our hot beverages. These are the single cup coffee makers that use K-Cups. I know a lot of other tiny house dwellers need their morning coffee, too. We decided to invest in a really nice kettle and use instant coffee. He likes the Starbucks Via brand because it doesn't taste like instant coffee. The kettle can be used for a number of purposes. Other options include:

- The smallest model of the Keurig.
- French press.
- Aeropress
- Becoming a regular at a local coffee shop.

62. Using Walls as Storage Space

Another great way to maximize your storage potential is to use all the vertical space possible. Use a magnetic knife strip on your wall. You can use hooks to hang your spoons, spatulas, and other utensils. Use a cork board to pin things to the wall to keep them off your tables and other surfaces. Use a chalk board to write notes rather than a pad of paper and a pen lying around the house. Creating shelves between the studs of your interior walls is another great way to maximize the space.

63. WATER IN THE UNPLUMBED TINY HOUSE

Lots of people ask us about our water system because we chose not to have running water or conventional plumbing in our tiny house. We decided to use the water from the spring that runs on our land. We collect that water and carry it up to the house in 4 gallon containers. Once there, we use a Big Berkey water filtration system to filter the water for household use. This water is used for showering, washing dishes, and drinking.

"The secret of happiness, you see, is not found in seeking more, but in developing the capacity to enjoy less." – Socrates

64. THE TINY SUMMER

For us, summer is all about celebration. Each year as we were building we hosted an Independence Day camp out over the 4th of July Weekend. Of course, 4th of July *is* Independence Day in the U.S., but the title has double meaning for us – building this tiny house gave us a new sense of independence in our lives.

Our tradition is to invite our friends to camp on our land. One year while we were still building the house I cooked several things at our apartment in Atlanta and froze them. They thawed in our cooler and I finished cooking them in our camp oven. One night we had camp nachos. The next night we enjoyed two different types of stuffed pasta shells. This wasn't your typical camp out. We played music and told stories around the camp fire.

Our first year officially living in the tiny house we were traveling near the 4th of July so we pushed our summer party back to later in the year. At this point the house was built, the outdoor kitchen was finished, and the Folk N' Ale (our "back yard" deck) became an outdoor stage. These are the kind of fantastic things you can do at your tiny house in the summer.

65. OUTDOOR LIVING SPACE

While we love living in our tiny house it is important to us to spend time outdoors as well. We really wanted to be able to maximize the 15 acres we own and enjoy the mountains and the woods.

Regardless of where you build your tiny house or where you park it, you will likely want to spend some of your time outdoors. You may be in someone's back yard or in a rural area, but make sure that you have a way to go outside and enjoy the area you're in from time to time.

Some ideas for outdoor living include:

- solar light decoration
- a porch or deck
- growing herbs
- a fire pit
- landscaping your tiny house
- gardening at your tiny house

66. THE BACONALIA

The ancient Romans celebrated the Bacchanalia in honor of
Bacchus, the god of wine. The idea of a bacon party came to us
while we were camping with friends. Late that week we
remembered that we had brought 2 pounds of bacon and we
really wanted to eat it, so we began to fry it. The sizzle and
aroma woke our camp mates and everyone was excited to get
their hands on some bacon as it came out of the pan. But that
much bacon generates a lot of grease. I said "what we need are
potatoes" and my friend said "I have potatoes!" So we cut them
up and threw them in the pan with some minced garlic and
cooked them for as long as it took for them to get perfectly
golden brown, tender and delicious. It is great for a celebration.
If you decide to have your own Baconalia, I recommend cooking
outside or using a splatter guard. Since it only uses one pan it is
a great idea for an outdoor tiny house party.

We use our Dutch oven because the deeper sides keep the
grease splatter to a minimum.

Start by frying your bacon. As you set bacon aside on paper towel to drain, don't be afraid to eat some as you continue to cook. That is part of the fun.

Once you've cooked a pound or so of bacon there should be quite a bit of grease in the pan.

Cut potatoes into thin slices. The thinner they are the faster they cook, but you don't want potato chip thin either. Maybe about a quarter to half an inch thick. Throw them in the grease and stir so everything is coated. Add some garlic or other seasoning as you choose. The bacon grease is very flavorful, however, so you don't need to do much. Let the potatoes cook until they are tender. This can take up to 40 minutes or so. Then remove them from the pan with a spatula and drain them on a paper towel and enjoy!

67. The Camp Chef Camp Oven (or Equivalent)

When I was introduced to the Camp Chef Camp Oven it changed the way I thought about cooking, camping, and living. The Camp Chef Camp Oven is designed for camping applications but we have found that it is a great addition to our tiny house. Since we chose not to install a traditional oven in our home, we use our camp oven to cook outside. The Camp Oven is propane powered, much like a traditional camp stove. You can simply screw in a one pound propane canister or use a larger tank with the regulator (available separately). The top of the camp oven is a two burner stove useful for typical stovetop recipes. The oven itself is easy to light and use.

Since it is a little more difficult to regulate the camp oven temperature than a household oven, it is best to leave the door closed as much as possible. If you need to make adjustments to the food during cooking or add any ingredients, simply remove the item from the oven and close the oven door to maintain the heat.

We have used our camp oven to cook casseroles, roast vegetables, and even bake. Smaller baking pans and cookie sheets work well for this small oven and for tiny house living in general.

.

68. CAMP NACHOS

I learned this recipe while we were building our tiny house. I would make it ahead of time and freeze it. It would thaw in the cooler while we worked on the house and I could cook it in the camp oven that evening.

Ingredients:

1lb Ground Chicken
1 tablespoon olive oil
Roasted Red Pepper Flake
Minced Garlic
1 packet taco seasoning
1 can black beans, drained
1 cup salsa
Shredded Mexican Cheese
Tortilla Chips
Sour Cream (optional)

Heat the oil in a skillet and add a healthy dose of roasted red pepper flakes and garlic. When the garlic starts to brown add the ground chicken. Break it up and let it cook through. Then add the taco seasoning. Mix thoroughly. Add the can of black beans, the cup of salsa, and stir. Let the mixture cool and transfer to the 6X6 pan (I use disposable foil pans). Cover in tin foil and freeze.

Once you are ready for dinner at your campsite, set up your Camp Chef Camp Oven and ignite. Set on high and wait for it to come to 350 degrees. Once it does, turn it down to low. Remove the foil from the nachos and place in oven. Monitor the oven to make sure the temperature stays at about 350 and adjust knob as necessary. Cook for about 20 to 30 minutes or until heated through. Add cheese to top of the nachos and place in oven again for about 10 minutes or until the cheese is melted and the nachos are bubbly. Serve on tortilla chips with a spoonful of sour cream or guacamole on top.

69. Landscaping the Tiny Space

Depending on where your tiny house is parked, you may wish to landscape your immediate area. If you are renting someone's back yard you can do this by adding planters with bright beautiful flowers around your house. Consider a removable window box so you always have a view of gorgeous flowers when you look outside.

You may create a path to your house using stone pavers or even wood chips.

If you are in a space where it is feasible you may wish to plant some trees.

70. An Outdoor Fire pit

When you have outdoor space it is nice to have a fire pit available for cooking or gathering. You can always build a simple rock ring or use a commercial brazier available at your local home improvement store. Here are the basics of a fire pit that we built.

We used stone pavers from the home improvement store. They are the kinds that are slightly tapered in so you can create curves. We began by laying down a layer of narrow, gray, open bricks in a rough circle to allow for airflow at the base of the fire. We then stacked two layers of the pavers on top to create the ring. We poured pea gravel in the bed of the fire pit to protect the ground. It was a simple job that only took a half a day. Make sure to level your ground before you begin. You can do this by digging a small pit and tamping it down.

Be safe when you build a fire. Don't over build and always have water available.

71. HERBS

When you do a lot of cooking it is nice to have fresh herbs at your disposal. If you have a tiny house, there are some great ways you can grow them yourself. You can have them as part of a garden or you can plant them in a small pot that stands on your porch. One idea is to plant herbs in tin cans or mason jars which can be attached to the side of your house and labeled. I like to have basil, cilantro, and rosemary on hand but you can choose whatever flavors you like the most. Consider buying a garden kit or individual potted herbs that you can replant at your tiny house. The rich green colors, scents, and flavors will enhance your entire tiny house experience.

72. Gardening

Learning to grow your own food is an easy fit within the tiny life experience. Many families and individuals are planting more of their own food in gardens and a tiny space is a perfect place to do that yourself. It goes hand in hand with self-sufficiency and sustainability.

As an alternative to a traditional garden try container or raised bed gardening to fit within your small yard.

73. GNOMES: TINY HOUSE PROTECTORS

Meet Chomsky.

Chomsky was a gift from my sister and her family. She felt we needed a tiny gnome for our tiny house. Our house would not be a home without Chomsky. I am so passionate about a gnome's place in a tiny house that I firmly believe everyone who builds one needs to acquire a gnome.

The best gnome for a tiny house?

You need to choose a gnome whose scale matches that of your home. If your home is on wheels make sure there is a secure place for him to travel indoors. Gnomes come in many colors and styles. Make sure to include your gnome in all your tiny house adventures.

74. OUTDOOR STORAGE

Outdoor storage can be very useful when living in a small space. You can use it for all of your tools and outdoor cooking utensils.

We have two forms of outdoor storage. One is the shelf beneath the outdoor kitchen. Since we collect all of our water from the spring, we have room for six 4-gallon containers of water out there. There is also a bin that holds all the outdoor cooking items including grill tools, lighters, fire starter, charcoal and wood chips for grilling along with dish soap and a brush for washing dishes. We store the camp oven in its case on this shelf.

We also built a "basement" below the house. Because our house is on cement piers, the back of the house sits quite a bit higher off the ground that the front. We used scrap lumber to build stepped platforms between three of the piers to make space to store some of our tools, shovels, hedge clippers, camp chairs and anything else that couldn't be stored indoors.

75. GARDEN INCINERATOR

When living off the grid something to consider is what is going to happen to your trash. Rather than sending it to a landfill, consider building a garden incinerator to dispose of any unwanted materials that are safe to burn.

The easiest way to do this is to buy a metal garbage can with a lid. You will also need a round grill grate that will fit in the bottom and three or four bricks.

Using a dremel tool or similar device, cut ventilation holes all the way around the bottom of the can. Place the bricks in the bottom and the grill grate on top of them. You can see how these ventilation holes will allow air to come up under the fire through the grate and continue to feed it oxygen. You then build the fire inside the incinerator. The fire will burn extremely hot so it will burn anything from fallen branches to paper trash quickly and efficiently.

76. COMPOSTING

Composting seems to go hand in hand with tiny house living. Many people who chose this lifestyle do so for the ecological impacts of reducing our carbon footprint and attempting to live more sustainably. Composting is one of the easiest ways you can accomplish this. I know many people living in conventional homes who also compost. There are two ways to do this.

- **Enclosed composting.** We chose to buy a commercial composting unit. It is a plastic barrel on a stand that you can rotate to process the materials inside as they compost. We did this primarily because of the possibility of bears on our mountain. We wanted the food waste to be concealed so they were less likely to attract animals.
- **Compost pile.** Building an exposed compost pile is just as easy. You can do this with chicken wire or old palates. The key is to keep the compost turning to continue to encourage the decomposition of the materials so it eventually becomes useful for gardening.

77. Outdoor Solar Lighting

You may want to consider solar lighting options for your outdoor space. The best part about solar decoration is that you are able to use them without worrying about electrical or battery power. Your local home and garden store should have lots of options.

- Garden Bulbs on stakes
- Hanging Lanterns
- Decorative solar statuary
- Landscape stakes

Whatever you decide to do, place your solar decoration with care. We decided to use some hanging lanterns placed in the trees above our outdoor deck to give some ambiance to the area at night. It wasn't enough to block out the stars, but offered a little mood lighting after the sun set.

78. Night Falls at the Tiny House

Have you ever sat back and watched bats at dusk? They flit across the tree line like shadows. It is so peaceful to sit out on a chair and tilt your head back to watch the bats as the sunset paints purple across the evening sky.

When the blue fades to purple then to violet and then finally the midnight blue of the night sky, only then will you begin to see the stars emerge. If it is a clear night, the constellations sketch across the sky leaving you with beautiful mythological stories to tell by the camp fire. You might catch a shooting star, a comet or a satellite if you are diligent enough.

Have you considered all the reasons you want to live simply? Now is the time to act on them.

"Home is the nicest word there is." —
Laura Ingalls Wilder

---

79. FAMILIES

Tiny house living sounds, on paper, like it would be best for only one person. I successfully live in a tiny space with my partner and we love every minute of it. It is quite possible to have a family in a tiny space. You may wish to have a home slightly larger than 120 square feet, but it is possible. Check out these tiny house families.

- Tiny House Family: www.tinyhousefamily.com
- Tiny r(E)volution: www.tinyrevolution.us
- Treading Tiny: www.treadingtiny.com

Andrew and Crystal Odom along with their daughter Tilly Madison. Photo courtesy of Tiny r(E)volution.

80. LOVE IN THE TINY HOUSE

Another common question we get asked is how exactly we can live in a tiny space with another person. Matt and I have been together since I was 19 years old. We enjoy each other's company a great deal and we are partners in everything. That isn't to say we don't disagree or even fight sometimes but we are pretty good at overcoming obstacles.

Living in the tiny house, however, was no obstacle. Now I find it strange to not be in the same room. I was lonely in the tiny house if I was by myself for extended periods of time. The key to living in a tiny space with another person is to really enjoy that other person's company.

Privacy is a big issue for some people. I know lots of people who have separate bathrooms or even bedrooms in their traditional homes. Neither of these are things we'd ever done before and saw no reason to start now. Downsizing into a wee house was a perfect fit for the way we already lived.

Photo by Andy Kalat

81. Tiny Entertaining

Entertaining in the tiny house can take on a lot of forms. Do you have just two people over for dinner on your outdoor deck? Do you invite all of your friends for a camping weekend with music and a campfire? Do you enjoy beer or wine or maybe a delicious cocktail like the one I describe in idea 84? (No peeking, you'll get there soon!)

Entertaining in the tiny house certainly requires some planning and space arrangements depending on your living situation and experience. However, I think it is important to entertain in your small space. Living in a different way like this should encourage us to engage with our lives and our friends and families.

82. GUESTS IN THE TINY HOUSE

You might think that you can't host people in your tiny house, but you would be wrong.

Because we have such a large area of land we often host camping events. We've had up to 12 people (about 6 tents) camping on our land. But recently we hosted an event where a good friend of ours stayed on the tiny futon in the tiny house. In the morning, as we made tea and looked out at the mists rising over the Smokey Mountains, she mused, "This is the way to wake up."

You may not be able to host scores of people at your tiny space, but with a little creativity you can create a memorable experience for your visitors.

83. Autumn at the Tiny House

Wherever you live, this time of year is blazing with reds and golds and it is as spectacular as you can imagine in the North Carolina Mountains. While spring is a time of action and rebirth, autumn is a time of reflection. For us, because we chose to leave the tiny house to travel for the winter, we considered the previous six months and how much we loved living in this way. It was bittersweet to leave, but exciting to know that we would be coming back as spring blooms on the mountain again. When you're engaged in the simple life the crisp autumn air and the explosion of color in the trees can give you a whole new perspective. Take this time to think about where you've been and where you want to go.

84. THE AUTUMNTINI

Even though I usually drink beer, I really wanted to include a cocktail recipe for the tiny house. This is the kind of drink you might have while you sit out on the deck watching the blazing orange sun set below the horizon of red leaves. I remembered this recipe we designed for a small Halloween party a few years ago. I didn't like the idea of all the kitschy horror themed drinks like "Vampire Blood" or "Witches' Brew," so this is what I came up with. It does involve making an infusion, so it requires some advanced preparation.

Add three cinnamon sticks to a bottle of vodka and store in the freezer. After about a week or so the flavor will be amazing.

In a martini shaker add:
Ice
One shot of Cinnamon infused vodka
One shot of crème de cacao
One shot of Bailey's Irish cream

Shake and pour into a martini glass through the strainer. Sprinkle ground cinnamon on top. You may also choose to rim the glass with cinnamon sugar.

85. KEEPING YOURSELF ENTERTAINED

One of the most common questions we are asked about life in the tiny house is how do we keep ourselves from getting bored. Truth is, I couldn't imagine getting bored in our house on the mountain since there are so many things to keep me engaged.

- Hiking our own land
- Hiking nearby trails
- Identifying trees, birds, and wildflowers
- Watching movies and TV via 4G Internet and a Tablet
- Listening to our iTunes music library
- Reading books on Kindle
- Relaxing outdoors
- Playing guitar and writing music
- Being part of our small town community
- Exploring other nearby towns
- Drinking beer
- Enjoying Great Smoky Mountains National Park
- Exploring the Blue Ridge Parkway
- Horseback riding at our neighbor's business
- Having friends visit from near and far
- Cooking
- Building campfires
- Outdoor adventures like rafting and canoeing
- Constructing creative things on our land
- Playing outdoor games like whiffle ball, ladder ball, bocce ball, and archery
- Throwing darts
- Gardening (we're not very good at it yet)
- Star gazing with the help of computer applications

- Playing online computer games with friends all over the country
- Shooting airsoft guns at aluminum cans
- Sometimes enjoying all that downtown Asheville has to offer

In addition to all of these fun things we've also grown to enjoy all of the chores that come with our off grid living situation. When you don't have to worry about driving to an office every day, things like carrying water and maintaining trails become enjoyable rather than tedious.

86. MUSIC IN THE TINY HOUSE

I love music and I was an early adopter of digital music. I am able to keep my entire collection of CDs and all the mixes I've put together over the years on a little device that fits easily in my purse or pocket.

For listening to music in the tiny house we purchased a small iPod dock where we can plug in our devices and listen to music all day. It can run on batteries or plug into our house. It doesn't use very much energy at all.

Another option would be satellite radio. Most satellite radio subscriptions include online streaming. I love listening to seasonal music. I also enjoy listening to NPR or other streaming radio in the tiny house. There is also an old timey device known as an FM radio.

Of course, you could always make your own music.

87. Room for all the Books

The best way to have your books in your tiny house is to convert them all to digital media. I know a lot of people have fears about getting rid of all of their paper books, but paper books and the extreme downsizing it takes to make it in a tiny house are not compatible. There are many options when it comes to book readers.

I use the Kindle app on an iPod Touch so I can hold it in one hand when I am reading. The other thing I really like about the Kindle app on the iPod touch is that I can read it in black text on a sepia background, which is easy on the eyes in the daylight, or I can read it in white text on a black background which is perfect for reading after dark. I have nearly forgotten what reading lamps are.

I remember a friend loaning me a paperback book recently. As I settled into bed for the night, I propped up my pillows and made myself comfortable. I grabbed the book off the night stand and...turned off the light. It took me a minute to realize what was wrong. And this part is going to freak out the bibliophiles in the audience: I never did read that paperback. I went back to the Kindle because it was much more convenient.

The Nook is another popular e-reader. It is produced by Barns and Noble and available in stores or online.

Both Barnes and Noble and Amazon offer great selections. I often browse the Amazon monthly feature "100 books for 3.99 or less" to get some great stuff.

CHAPTER II

SHOES IN THE ROAD

I

They reached the shoes at mid-morning. Beyond them, clearer now, stood the glass palace. It glimmered a delicate green shade, like the reflection of a lily pad in still water. There were shining gates in front of it; red pennons snapped from its towers in a light breeze.

The shoes were also red.

Susannah's impression that there were six pairs was understandable but wrong—there were actually four pairs and one quartet. This latter—four dark red booties made of supple leather—was undoubtedly meant for the four-footed member of their ka-tet. Roland picked one of them up and felt inside it. He didn't know how many bumblers had ever been gifted with a set of silk-lined leather booties, but he was willing to guess that none had ever worn shoes in the history of the world.

"Bally, Gucci, eat your heart out," Eddie said. "This is great stuff."

Susannah's were easiest to pick out, and not just because of the feminine, sparkly swoop on the sides. They weren't really shoes at all—they had been made to fit over the stumps of her legs, which ended just above the knees.

"Now look at this," she marvelled, holding one up so the sun could flash on the rhinestones with which the shoes were decorated . . . if they were rhinestones. She had a crazy notion that maybe they were diamond chips. "Capplies. After four years of gettin along in what my friend Cynthia calls 'circumstances of reduced leg-room,' I finally got myself a pair of capplies. Think of that."

"Capplies," Eddie mused. "Is that what they call 'em?"

"That's what they call em, sugar."

Jake's were bright red Oxfords—except for the color, they would have looked perfectly at home in the well-bred classrooms of the Piper School. He flexed one, then turned it over. The sole was bright and unmarked. There was no manufacturer's stamp, nor had he really expected one. His father had maybe a dozen pairs of fine handmade shoes.

Eddie's were low boots with Cuban heels (Maybe in this world you call them Mejis heels, he thought) and pointed toes . . . what, back in his other life, had been known as "street boppers." Kids from the midsixties—an era Odetta/Detta/Susannah had just missed—might have called them "fuzzie boots."

Roland's, of course, were cowboy boots. Fancy ones—you'd go dancing rather than droving in such as these. Looped stitching, side decorations, narrow, haughty arches. He examined them without picking them up, then looked at his fellow travellers and frowned. They were looking at each other. You would have said three people couldn't do that, only a pair . . . but you only would have

The difference between friends and pets is that friends we allow into our company, pets we allow into our solitude. - Robert Brault

---

88. Pets in Tiny Spaces

We might be best known on the internet for our cat, Piglet. She has become a poster child for pets in tiny houses. Upon moving into the tiny house Piglet demanded that we make certain concessions and we obliged. There are many things to consider when it comes to having a cat in your tiny space. I imagine dogs could make things even more complicated with the potential need for doggy doors and they may never get up to the loft. Here are some of the things we needed to consider for Piglet.

- Outdoor Spaces
- Loft Access
- Toys
- Litter Box Access

89. Outdoor Spaces for your Furry Friends

I am not an advocate of allowing cats outdoors to roam free. I think it is too dangerous with disease, cars, strangers, and other animals to contend with. Piglet, for various reasons, is indoor only. But she does like to go outside. We do this by taking her for "walks" on her leash. Yes, you can leash train a cat if you start when they are kittens. Often the cat is the one who take the lead. We say that we are taking Piglet on a "Follow." This keeps her active and her mind stimulated. Another option is to build an enclosure for the cat to be outside safely. There are also commercially available cat enclosure options. If you don't have a fenced yard for your dog you may consider a yard stake to clip their leash to in order to keep them safe.

90. Loft Access for Pets

The biggest puzzle we had to piece together upon moving into the little house was how to get Piglet up to the loft. We thought she might learn to use the ladder but she wanted nothing to do with it the first time she spent the night there. So, we devised a series of platforms.

We used traditional shelving brackets which allowed us to adjust the height as Piglet became comfortable with the arrangement. We installed two shelves that make it easy for Piglet to jump to the loft. We covered the platforms with pieces of FLOR carpet tiles, which gives Piglet a soft place to stand but also provides scratching options for her. FLOR is more durable than regular carpet and, as an added bonus, is a great scratcher.

On the first day we showed Piglet how to use the platforms and she seemed to get it, but that night she didn't come up to the loft. When I went down in the middle of the night I stopped to give her a smooch where she was sleeping on the couch and reminded her that she could use the platforms to get to the bed. Matt heard our midnight exchange and called her name from the loft. A light bulb went off in her little head and she hopped right up.

Over time, Piglet not only learned how to use those platforms to get up to the storage loft as well but she also figured out how to climb the ladder – a daily event that never stops being fun to watch.

91. Laser Pointer and Other Toys

Cats need lots of exercise and in the case of Piglet, who is exceptionally smart, lots of stimulation to keep them from going absolutely nuts. No one ever told Piglet she should be nocturnal so she sleeps with us all night long. We prefer that she not have a lot of pent up energy before bed or we don't get to sleep right away. One solution, besides occasional walks on her leash, was to get a laser pointer. It is a great toy for a small space and very entertaining to watch.

Other great toys for small spaces like the tiny house are cat dancers (toys on a stick or string) and a wrestling toy so she can grab on, bite, and kick with her back feet.

92. LITTER BOXES IN SMALL SPACES

Since Piglet is an indoor only cat we needed to make sure she had a place for her litter box that was out of the way for us but convenient for her. Our solution was to create a small access door in one of the tiny closets where we would then place the litter box. We framed it out so that it was slightly bigger than the opening of her covered litter box. It is finished the same way as the rest of the wall with trim around the edges to give it a complete look. We placed a small piece of the FLOR on the inside of the framing to keep litter tracking to a minimum and another just outside the litter box door to provide the same thing. Piglet immediately understood the process and finds it quite comfortable. We like the fact that the litter box is out of the way but we have easy access for cleaning it.

"Perfection is achieved, not when there is nothing more to add, but when there is nothing left to take away." – Antoine de Saint-Exupe

---

93. Window Treatments

Window treatments in your tiny house may depend on the area in which you've built or parked your home. Our home is in the middle of the woods so we are unconcerned with window treatments of any sort. However, there are several options you can consider.

- Pull down shades
- Mini blinds
- Curtains
- Shutters
- Roman shades

94. Closet Storage

The tiny house that we chose to build, the Tumbleweed Tiny House Company "Tarleton" design, included two small closets on either side of the front door. In our configuration, obviously, Matt gets one and I get the other. Matt built a two tiered shelf system for both closets. The middle shelf is for shoes and the top shelves hold stackable organizers from the Container Store. We chose a 4 tier system for each closet and we have more than enough storage space for all of our clothes.

95. CURTAINS AS CLOSET DOORS

When we were thinking about how to build closet doors for our tiny house we decided that curtains were the best available option. Because our house is designed to have a front door in the center and two small closets on either side closet doors seemed not only difficult to build but difficult to use. There would be times when we both needed to be in our closets with the doors open. The closet doors were also likely to block the front door. By installing a header on the top of the closet area we were able to hide a small tension rod to hang the curtain. We chose canvas style curtains. This is an attractive and easy way to solve the problem of the closet doors.

96. Using Color in Your Tiny Space

Your tiny house is a reflection of your personality. Decorate in a way that makes you happen. Color is a great way to do that. Matt and I opted for pine siding inside the house and we accented it with leaf green and mountain gray accents. There is so much you can do to customize your tiny house to fit your personal style.

- Imagine a tiny house in fall colors with darker brown wood, reds and oranges. Some people suggest not using dark colors, but it depends on what you like. It might make the room look smaller, but it will also make it look warmer.
- Decorate your tiny house in all white with a few splashes of red or blue to accent. These surprises will draw your eyes to them. The Tennessee Tiny Homes Company uses this technique in their custom buildings.
- Go shabby chic with a rainbow of beautiful reclaimed pieces. Some older furniture was built on a smaller scale and can fit into a tiny house without any modification. Take a paint brush to anything that needs a little cleaning up.

97. CEILING TREATMENTS

Some people choose the same treatment for their ceiling as their walls, but this isn't necessary. Here are some other ideas.

- **Decorative Tin Tiles.** These tiles can often be found in junk shops or salvage yards. They can be painted or finished or simply epoxied to keep the aged patina they will likely have when you find them. You can also buy new ones in many styles at your local home improvement store.
- **Fabric.** You can keep the rafters of the tiny house exposed and drape the area with decorative fabric to give the house a gypsy wagon effect.
- **Salvage material.** Salvage yards and thrift stores are great places to find ceiling coverings. In such a tiny space it is worth being creative. You can use anything from barn wood to old windows.

98. Adding Fabrics to your Design

Using fabrics in your tiny home can add a touch of comfort and class. I briefly mentioned fabrics for ceiling treatments, but there are many places you can use them in your home. When thinking about what fabrics make the most sense you will need to consider how they will be used. Delicate fabrics make little sense on seating that will be used daily and harsh wool might not make the best blanket. Think about these applications.

- Upholstery
- Window Treatments
- Bedding
- Additional accents such as pillows and throws

Consider your color scheme and what you want to accent. We decided our color scheme would be green and gray so we selected a tiny gray sofa and accented it with bright green pillows and blankets which match the stain we of our countertops.

Other options for fantastic fabrics include

- Tie dye
- Toile patterns
- Velvet
- Corduroy and denim
- Plaids

99. ADDING RUGS

Many people choose some type of wood flooring for their tiny home. Depending on how you have constructed your home you may find that the bare floors are chilly on your toes in the cold mornings. Here are two suggestions for rugs in your tiny home.

- **Throw Rugs**

Rugs like this are ubiquitous when you think of supplemental floor coverings. Matching a throw rug to your décor is easy and you can place the rug near your entry way, in your living space, or in your kitchen. They are easy to move when the floor needs to be cleaned and are typically machine washable.

- **FLOR**

FLOR is a carpet tile with a rubberized backing that makes it easy to install any space. We chose to use this in both of our lofts and matched it to the color green that we used throughout. We also covered the rungs in our ladder and the two cat platforms because its surface is excellent for our cat to scratch.

100. Lighting in the Tiny House

It is important to have the right lighting in your tiny house but it doesn't take nearly as many fixtures as a conventionally sized home. The typical types of lighting you want in a home are task lighting and overhead lighting. Decorative lighting is not necessary in such a tiny space unless you really want it.

I would suggest that table lamps are not the best use of space. A floor lamp might work depending on where you place it in your layout. One overhead light, a reading light, a dining table light, a kitchen light, and a bathroom light should be all you need. If you don't want to wire those into your tiny home hanging lamps that plug in would also work.

Ikea has a great selection of lighting fixtures that will fit comfortably into a tiny house. The style will depend on your overall design. Sleek modern fixtures or rustic cabin fixtures would complement many tiny house styles.

May health, peace, and sweet content be yours. – William Shakespeare

101. Dealing with Rain

There is nothing more relaxing than lying in the loft hearing the gentle spring rains fall softly on the metal roof. Our ceiling is well insulated so we don't have that hard water-on-metal sound that people associate with tin roofs, although I find that sound soothing as well. However, not every rainstorm is gentle. It can be a little nerve-wracking to be in a tiny space when a storm is raging around you. And when that storm hits, there isn't much you can do about it. It is worse when you need to get down the mountain to your car and realized your umbrellas are in that very car you're heading toward. That is when you improvise. Plastic trash bags make for excellent ponchos – though you will look like a dork.

Staying safe is important so make sure you have a safety plan that fits your tiny house situation. So far we haven't needed to take any drastic measures. The biggest problem we've ever had was dealing with the mud in the aftermath.

102. MUD!

Mud in your tiny house is no fun but when you live remotely like we do it is inevitable. If you can, take your wet coat and shoes off on the porch and leave them there. This isn't always going to work if the rain is still blowing sideways. Have a small rug inside the door to set your muddy shoes on when you remove them. Constant sweeping will keep the dirt at bay on the floor, but the only real solution to the mud is to clean the floors on your hands and knees. Sure you can invest in a mop or one of those Swiffer floor cleaners but in a tiny space there may not be a convenient space to store them. Cleaning the floor on your hands and knees isn't so bad when the space is so small. The only way to avoid it is to never wear muddy shoes inside.

I also recommend investing in a good boot scraper for your tiny porch or steps. This way, even when it isn't raining, you can clean off your shoes before stepping inside to take them off. We have a two-step approach. We use the boot scraper first to remove the worst of the dirt from our shoes. Then we wipe our shoes a second time on the welcome mat before stepping into the house.

103. CLEANING UP AFTER YOURSELF

There is a simple fact of life when you live in a tiny house in the woods; we have to sweep a lot. Because the house is so small it is quick and easy to sweep. One of the primary advantages of downsizing in such an extreme way is that cleaning never takes very long. No matter how dirty it gets cleaning our kitchen takes about ten minutes. Cleaning the bathroom is even quicker. We have a small vacuum but only use it to vacuum the FLOR in the loft or the stray litter that Piglet tracks out of her box. Cleaning the tiny house is really simple and can even be relaxing.

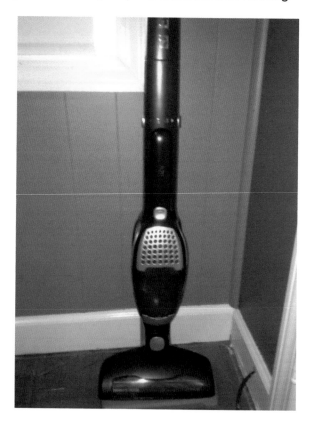

104. Do Your Chores

Depending on how you've built your tiny house or whether or not you are off the grid, you will have various chores throughout the day. I have never been a chore driven person. I don't enjoy that kind of thing and really; who does? But living in the tiny house changed my perspective on some things. Of course, since we gather our water from a spring and we live off the grid our chores are quite different from other tiny house builders, but here is a snapshot of what I do on a typical day.

- **Fill the water filter.** Our Berkey water filter is large and cumbersome so I had to figure out the best way to fill it. I saved a 1 gallon water jug and marked it with the words "Berkey Water." I fill that up with spring water and bring it into the house and pour into the Berkey. The Berkey holds a little more than two gallons at a time so some days I only have to fill it up with one gallon and some days I make two trips.

- **Empty the gray water.** We only have one drain in our entire house and it's in the shower. Underneath the house we put two screws on a floor joist next to the drain to act as hooks for a 5 gallon bucket. Every day I take that bucket down and walk over the gray water reclamation system we built to empty it. Then I replace the bucket. I try to do this every day so the bucket doesn't get too full and too heavy to carry.

- **Regular household tasks.** Water related chores are certainly specific to me, but there are other things that just about any tiny house owner needs to take care of. It is always a good idea to do these things right away so stuff doesn't get piled up. Do all of the dishes after every meal. Sweep the floor every time you see that it needs it. And make sure to scoop that litter box daily.

105. LAUNDRY

People ask us all the time about how we do laundry in the tiny house since we don't have running water. We do know tiny house builders that included small stackable washer and dryer units in their homes, but we chose not to do this since we didn't want to plumb the house traditionally. We knew all along that we planned to use a Laundromat to wash our clothes.

What we couldn't have imagined was how lucky we would be in this arena just because we chose to live near Asheville, NC. After moving to the area, we started doing laundry at a small Laundromat that was reasonably close to our tiny house. I found this chore stunningly boring. When we lived in conventional homes and apartments I hated laundry. I tended to live out of my laundry basket because once something was washed and dried, I had no desire to fold and put away. The Laundromat forced me to do this step just to transport the clean clothes to the tiny house, but I still hated it.

Then we heard about **Bar of Soap** – a Laundromat bar in North Asheville. What an amazing concept! Suddenly we really enjoyed laundry. A chore that seemed to take infinite time now seems to wiz by. We are able to start our washing machines, order our first beer and enjoy it while talking to folks at the bar. When the first beer is done, we can put our clothes in the dryer and enjoy a second beer. When the beer is done so is our laundry. Then we fold up our clothes and head back to the mountain. I look forward to laundry every week now because it has become a strangely social activity.

Photo by Jeff Priskorn

Of course, once we are back in the tiny house the clothes get put away immediately so they don't create clutter.

106. A TINY TOUCH

I love fun little surprises in the tiny house. While most of what we own is practical there are a few little pieces here and there that are just placed for fun.

- **Tiny Element.** My Honda Element is the unsung hero in our building journey. I have a little match box car to match it. This sits in a small recess at the top of the wall.
- **Tiny Beer Glasses.** Beer Festivals are a favorite pastime of ours. From each event we have acquired a single 4 ounce beer taster. We have 5 that we've kept and they are sitting on a shelf in the tiny house. Plus, they are occasionally functional since we use them for wine glasses.
- **Gnomes.** We have Chomsky outside, but inside we have a pair of gnomes that were given to us as a gift when we moved in.
- **Decorative Plaque.** Another friend gave us a small tile with a Shakespeare quote. We hung this on the door inside the tiny house.

Decorating with a few tiny items brings really makes the tiny house feel like our home.

107. REAL LIFE STORAGE IDEAS

It seems like so many of the ideas in this book are about storage of one sort or another. For tiny house living to be successful everything in the house needs a proper place. There are many types of storage you can have in your tiny house and most people use a combination of things.

- Drawers
- Built In shelves
- Storage Boxes
- Cabinets
- Closet organizers

We decided not to use built in drawers for anything in our tiny house but many other tiny house builders have done this successfully. Instead we put together two commercially available drawer units to fit inside the smaller of our kitchen cabinets. In these drawers we store all of our kitchen utensils as well as our coffee and hot cocoa needs. We also built shelves into the interior wall studs to store some additional small items. Our storage loft has a combination of decorative storage boxes for additional items.

108. Staircases vs. Ladder: The Debate Over Lofts

There has been much debate within the tiny house community over which is better: lofts or first floor bedrooms. You can read about the options on so many of the tiny house community blogs. There are choices every tiny homeowner needs to make. Do you prefer a sturdy staircase over a ladder? Do you have room for a bed on the first level? Each has its pros and cons which I want to explore in a little more detail in the following ideas.

109. Staircases

If you have a slightly larger tiny house you may want to consider stairs. Several companies are making stairs that have alternating steps which keep the staircase narrower to fit in a smaller space. Additionally you can use stairs that have drawers built into the steps which will not only solve the staircase issue but also maximize your storage space. There are also some innovative corner staircase designs that might work in the right space. If you have the additional space you may want to consider a small spiral staircase.

110. LADDER

If you have a tiny house with a sleeping loft, you will likely need a ladder to access it. There are many ways to make your own ladder or you could buy something commercially made that will work well. Our ladder was simple construction from 2X4s and each rung was covered in the FLOR carpet tiles that we used in both lofts. Even our cat has learned to navigate the ladders. It is also movable so we can access both the sleeping loft and the storage loft. We put J hooks on the front of each of the lofts and eye hooks on the ladder so it could be moved back and forth easily.

Other options for your tiny ladders include:

- Metal ladder
- Library ladder with wheels to move out of the way of your living space
- Folding ladder like the kind you might use for an attic
- Ladder built into a bookshelf

111. THE LOFT

When you build a tiny home you will need to consider how you want to design your sleeping loft. There were several things that went into our decision. We used a square awning style window in the loft gable. We chose to use a futon mattress which fit perfectly in the space. We also chose to carpet the space using a product called FLOR. This is what makes our tiny loft very cozy and homey.

We ran electrical wiring to outlets on either side of the bed as well as a three way switch so we could turn the main overhead light off from there or the main floor.

You will spend a lot of time in your loft and you want to make sure that your experience up there is comfortable. Surround yourself with warm comforters and soft pillows. Next thing you know, you and your cat will doze there for hours.

112. THE FIRST FLOOR BEDROOM

When a lot of people look into tiny houses they become concerned about having to access lofts, especially as they get older. Others are looking for better accessibility due to a disability. Many more people might choose tiny living if they could have a first floor bed. While the most popular style of tiny house does feature a loft there are many ways to design small spaces with first floor access.

Tiny homes based on trailer designs can be easily made to have a downstairs bedroom.

Tumbleweed Tiny House Company has a several of styles of small and tiny homes and cottages with first floor bedrooms.

You may also wish to consider working with a designer to see what would be a good fit for you and the space you want to ultimately build.

A simple solution would also be to use convertible furniture such as a futon in your primary living space.

"A good traveler has no fixed plans, and is not intent on arriving." - Lao Tzu

113. TINY WINTER TIME

People are surprised to hear that we don't live in our tiny house over the winter. We specifically chose that path since our new lives were as much about location independence as they are about living in a tiny space. Living in a tiny house reduced our expenses enormously and gave us the flexibility to be where we want when we want. Because of this, we have the opportunity to spend quite a bit of time with family over the holidays and do a lot of traveling.

However, tiny houses can and should be built to sustain the winters.

After you've insulated and heated the tiny home properly, buy yourself a cozy comforter, plenty of flannel pajamas and warm socks, and you'll be just fine. Imagine sitting in your tiny space with a cup of hot cocoa watching the snow drift to the ground.

114. How to Heat Your Tiny House

Heating the tiny house is a cause for great debate among builders. There are so many potential solutions that there really isn't one best way to do it. We chose not to install a conventional heat source directly into our home. Our home is in the south and our winters are mild and short. Rather than installing a permanent heater, we use a portable ventless propane heater that is designed for camping. Because our house is well insulated, and tiny, it works well to heat the space. We have plenty of safety measures in place including a carbon monoxide detector and oxygen sensor. We always keep a couple of windows cracked to ensure adequate ventilation.

However, most tiny house builders chose to use some form of built in heating. Tiny homes use very little energy to heat because of their size and if they are insulated well they will trap the heat for a long time. Safety is important for all heating options so be sure to do your homework before you install anything. Some options for heaters include:

- **Wood stove.** This is a great source of heat for a small space because you won't use much wood. If your tiny house is in a natural setting like ours you may have an unlimited supply. There are very tiny wood stoves available that can easily fit within a small space.
- **Propane stove.** The Tumbleweed Tiny House Company suggests a product called the Newport Propane Fireplace designed specifically for boats and small homes. It is a cozy looking little device that puts out quite a bit of heat and gives you a fireplace-like ambiance.

- **Electric Space Heaters.** There are several types of heaters that would work if you have access to the electrical grid. Keep in mind, however, that when solar power converts anything to heat it uses much more energy and becomes less efficient.
- **Infrared Heater.** This is another type of electric powered heater that is very efficient compared to their radiant counterparts. Several models are considered "Eco" for up to 500 square feet.

115. INSULATING THE TINY SPACE

It is important to insulate your tiny house well. Regardless of where in the world you've built it will need to stay cool in the summer and warm in the winter. The right insulation can make all the difference. There are several options.

- Extruded foam board
- Expanded foam board
- Fiberglass insulation
- Denim or cotton insulation
- Blown insulation

Determine what works best for your tiny home and be sure to install it properly.

116. Happy Holidays

Matt and I love to decorate for the holidays. Before moving into the tiny house we decorated every room of our conventional house. We would start on the first of October and keep the Halloween decorations up until we could replace them with Thanksgiving decorations. As soon as Thanksgiving was over, the traditional winter holiday decorations came out. Since moving into the tiny house we've had to scale back but we aren't willing to give up the tradition.

Halloween is our favorite so we have amassed a large collection of Halloween decorations over the years. Those were some of the hardest things to get rid of when we began to downsize. For the tiny house in the woods we like a more rustic look. We decorate our Folk N' Ale with bales of hay, scarecrows and pumpkins. Spooky lights add a creepy touch to the season.

For the winter holidays, we have a tiny tinsel tree decorated with beautiful hand blown glass ornaments. Each ornament represents a different aspect of ancient Greek mythology – something that we are both very interested in . It fits up on the storage loft and the white lights practically illuminate the entire house.

117. JERK SHRIMP AND NOODLES

For tiny living and outdoor cooking it is great to have simple recipes with two or three ingredients. For this meal all you need are shrimp, a Jamaican jerk marinade, and angel hair pasta.

I started by marinating the shrimp in the jerk sauce for probably about `10 minutes or so while I boiled the angel hair. Once the angel hair was done, I drained it and set it aside. I threw the shrimp in a skillet. I chose frozen cooked shrimp but you could use either cooked or raw - just make sure the shrimp is nice and pink and you'll know it is done.

After I was happy with the shrimp, I threw the pasta in the pan to cook in the sauce, tossing it with tongs to get it coated. If you want a little extra kick, which I do sometimes, you can add some crushed red pepper flakes as well.

It won't take long for the pasta to be coated with the sauce and once that is done, the dish is ready. It is super quick and really easy to prepare, even in a very tiny off the grid kitchen.

118. TRAVELING

The beauty of tiny living is simplifying your life enough to have all the tools you need to enjoy it on your own terms. One of the benefits of tiny living for us is the ability to travel.

If you have a house on a foundation like ours you can't take it with you. Instead we live our lives in a location independent way. By having a flexible freelance job that I can do from anywhere in the world I am able to go wherever I want whenever I want and I'm still able to generate an income. In the summer we spent three weeks traveling, including a week at a camping festival. And we spent time with family and friends in Michigan for two months over the holidays.

If your tiny house is on a trailer it can join you on your adventures. Many campgrounds allow tiny houses but some do not. Do your research ahead of time to make sure that you are welcome. If you have friends or family all over the country you may be able to take your tiny house with you as you visit. Keep in mind that a tiny house isn't designed the same way as a travel trailer so tiny house builders don't recommend driving with it frequently. If you do want to move your tiny house on a regular basis you may need to do some additional work to keep it road worthy.

119. Simple Living

Simple living isn't just about living in a tiny space. This is something that everyone can do wherever they are. Many of the tips we've covered already are a great way to change the way you interact with your living space right now.

Many aspects of simple living became more important once I moved into the tiny house. They include:

- **Location Independence.** As I mentioned, this is the ability to earn a living from anywhere in the world.
- **Simple eating.** Farmer's markets and other changes in our food buying habits made our entire eating experience very different. This means that we shop more often but eat more healthy foods.
- **Less stuff.** The fewer things I have to worry about the less stressed I am. The formula is simple. This doesn't mean I want to discard everything. In fact, some devices make the tiny life much easier. But overall we have a one in, one out policy meaning we have to discard anything we are no longer using as soon as we have the urge to replace it.

120. Tiny House Community

One of my dreams for the future of tiny homes is to see more people create tiny house communities. There are many ways to make this possible.

Imagine getting together with some of your best friends or members of your family. Pool your resources to buy several acres of land and build individual tiny homes. Depending on the dynamics of your group you may wish to share some spaces such as kitchen, dining, and recreational areas.

Another option is to build a tiny house rental community. Many cities are starting to allow pocket neighborhoods. These infill developments could be an answer to urban density issues throughout the country.

What about an intentional community? Back in the 60s many people would have called this a commune, but the concept has changed. Develop a community based on shared values and centered around cooperation. This kind of community space is where you can really get to know your neighbors. Maybe you can start a small community garden where everyone can pitch in and take some of the harvest. Maybe it is a great way to have an artist community. The possibilities are endless.

We were born to unite with our fellow men, and to join in community with the human race.

-- Cicero

143

Most of the ideas in this book were pulled from my own experience but there is a flourishing Tiny House community all over the United States and throughout the world. Many of these people share their own unique stories in books, videos, and websites.

For more inspiration here are some other tiny house blogs that I recommend.

- Tiny r(E)volution: www.tinyrevolution.us
- The Tiny Life: www.thetinylife.com
- Tiny House Talk: www.tinyhousetalk.com
- Tiny House Listings: www.tinyhouselistings.com
- Rowdy Kittens: www.rowdyskittens.com
- Smalltopia: www.loganblairsmith.com
- Tiny House News: www.tinyhousenews.info
- Tiny House Ontario: www.tinyhouseontario.com
- Tiny House Swoon: www.tinyhouseswoon.com
- Relax Shacks: www.relaxshacks.blogspot.com
- Tumbleweed Tiny House Company: www.tumbleweedtinyhouses.com
- Four Lights Tiny House Company: www.fourlightstinyhouses.com
- Mini Motives: www.minimotives.com
- Treading Tiny: www.treadingtiny.com
- Trying on Tiny: www.tryingontiny.com
- Tiny Tack House: www.chrisandmalissa.com

The list above is filled with great stories, advice, tips, and tricks. Still, there is only so much reading you can do. Eventually you just have to build. The most important step to any of this is to start. Here is where I tell you to put down this book and go live your dream, whatever it looks like.

I would rather regret the things that I have done than the things that I have not.
--Lucille Ball

Laura M. LaVoie is a freelance writer and blogger living in a 120 Square Foot Cabin with her partner, Matt, and their Sphynx cat, Piglet. Laura and Matt built the tiny house with their own hands after researching several types of alternative building techniques including Cordwood Masonry and Earthships. They decided on a small house because the Tiny House Movement matched their values and lifestyle perfectly. They began building the house in the mountains of North Carolina in 2009 and construction took three years as they lived and worked in Atlanta and would travel and build on weekends. Now Laura,

Matt, and Piglet live and work in the tiny house full time. Follow their blog Life in 120 Square Feet at www.120squarefeet. com for more about their tiny lifestyle.

The tiny house has been featured in Huffington Post, CNN iReport, The Laurel of Asheville and a number of tiny house community websites including the Tumbleweed Tiny House website.

When not building or living in a tiny house, Laura enjoys brewing and drinking craft beer and spending time in downtown Asheville, NC.

28193295R00081

Made in the USA
Lexington, KY
08 December 2013